Enemies
of
Slavery

by DAVID A. ADLER

illustrated by

DONALD A. SMITH

HOLIDAY HOUSE / New York

To Joe and Judy,
Jeffrey and David
D. A. A.

To Mary and all those who care about the human spirit
D. A. S.

The heroes profiled here were selected only as examples
of the many brave and diverse heroes who fought for emancipation.

"God will not make his face shine upon a nation
that holds with slavery."—Sojourner Truth, 1850

In 1619 twenty or so African blacks were brought to Jamestown, Virginia, and sold
as indentured servants, slaves for a limited time. Later, thousands more were brought
in chains to the American colonies, but the terms of their service changed. They and any
children born to them were slaves for life, considered the "property" of their "owners."
By 1861, the beginning of the Civil War, there were 4 million slaves in the United States.
In 1863 Abraham Lincoln's Emancipation Proclamation declared all slaves in the
Confederate states to be free; but those states were in rebellion, not really subject to the
proclamations of the president. The end of slavery in the United States came
in December 1865 with the passage of the Thirteenth Amendment.

Text copyright © 2004 by David A. Adler
Illustrations copyright © 2004 by Donald A. Smith
All Rights Reserved
Printed in the United States of America
www.holidayhouse.com
First Edition
1 3 5 7 9 10 8 6 4 2

Library of Congress Cataloging-in-Publication Data
Adler, David A.
Enemies of slavery / by David A. Adler; illustrated by Donald A. Smith.
p. cm.
Includes bibliographical references.
ISBN 0-8234-1596-1
1. Abolitionists—United States—Biography—Juvenile literature.
2. Antislavery movements—United States—History—Juvenile literature.
3. Slavery—United States—History—Juvenile literature.
4. African Americans—History—To 1863—Juvenile literature.
I. Smith, Donald A., 1934– II. Title.
E449.A1556 2004
326'.8'092273—dc22
2003062548

Contents

John Brown
(1800–1859)

"I, John Brown, am now quite certain that the crimes of this
guilty land will never be purged away but with blood."
—*from Brown's last written statement, December 2, 1859*

When John Brown was twelve, he saw a black slave severely beaten.
Right then he declared an eternal war with slavery. Brown's war
would be a bloody war.

In 1856 he led an attack that killed five unarmed proslavery set-
tlers. He did this to get even with the proslavery side for their
assault on Lawrence, Kansas, an antislavery city. Three years later,
on Sunday, October 16, 1859, Brown and his followers raided and
took over a government weapons storehouse in Harpers Ferry,
Virginia (now West Virginia). Brown planned to begin a revolt that
would free the slaves, using these weapons, but by Tuesday they had
lost the storehouse and his war.

Brown was caught, tried, and sentenced to hang by a noose made
of cotton picked by the very slaves he had hoped to free. Among
the fifteen hundred soldiers who gathered to watch his execution
were Stonewall Jackson, one of the South's greatest generals, and
John Wilkes Booth, who in 1865 would murder President Abraham
Lincoln.

Frederick Douglass
(1817 or 1818–1895)

"I often found myself regretting my own existence and
wishing myself dead; and but for the hope of being free, I
have no doubt but that I should have killed myself."
—from Douglass's autobiography, 1845

In his autobiography, Frederick Douglass wrote of Edward Covey, his cruel master who "tore off my clothes, lashed me till he had worn out his switches." And there was no getting away from Covey. "He was under every tree, behind every stump, in every bush, and at every window on the plantation. . . . The thoughts of being *a slave for life* began to bear heavily upon my heart."

In 1838 Douglass escaped and moved north.

Douglass's house became a "station" on the Underground Railroad—a safe house for runaway slaves. He lectured widely about the evils of slavery, and then published a newspaper of his own, the *North Star*. Douglass was a powerful voice for abolition—the ending of slavery.

"Go where you may, search where you will, roam through all the monarchies and despotisms of the old world," Douglass said in an 1852 speech in Rochester, New York, "and you will say with me, that, for revolting barbarity and shameless hypocrisy, America reigns without rival."

William Lloyd Garrison
(1805–1879)

"Let all the enemies of the persecuted blacks tremble."
—*from the first issue of Garrison's* Liberator, *1831*

"In the name of God who has made us of one blood," William Lloyd Garrison said in an 1842 Independence Day speech in Boston, "I demand the immediate emancipation of those who are pining in slavery on the American soil."

Garrison's demands were published monthly beginning in January 1831 in the *Liberator,* the weekly antislavery newspaper he and Isaac Knapp founded. "I will be as harsh as truth and uncompromising as justice," Garrison wrote in the first issue. "I am in ernest [*sic*]; I will not equivocate; I will not excuse; I will not retreat a single inch—AND I WILL BE HEARD." He called slavery "an earthquake rumbling under our feet . . . a national catastrophe . . . a combination of Death and Hell."

Garrison's newspaper was an earthquake rumbling too, a weekly cry that was not stilled until 1865, when this nation's slaves were set free.

Abraham Lincoln
(1809–1865)

"I do order and declare that all persons held as slaves within said designated states and parts of states are, and henceforward shall be, free."

—*from Lincoln's* Emancipation Proclamation, *which declared all slaves in sections of the United States then in rebellion to be free, January 1, 1863*

"A house divided against itself cannot stand," Abraham Lincoln said in June 1858. "I believe this government cannot endure, permanently, half slave and half free."

That year, Lincoln was the Republican Party candidate for the United States Senate. In a debate with Senator Stephen A. Douglas, the Democratic Party candidate, Lincoln said, "There is no reason in the world why the Negro is not entitled to all natural rights enumerated in the Declaration of Independence—the right to life, liberty, and the pursuit of happiness." Lincoln's words frightened slaveholders.

Abraham Lincoln lost the 1858 Senate election, but in 1860 he was elected president of the United States. In the wake of his election, a man many people considered an enemy of slavery, the legislatures of seven Southern states voted to withdraw from the Union. They formed the Confederate States of America.

"I hold that, in contemplation of universal law and of the Constitution," Lincoln said, "the Union of these states is perpetual"—no state had the right to secede. Many Southerners considered his speech an act of war. One month later, there *was* war. Four more states joined the Confederacy. The Civil War ended in April 1865 with the surrender of the Confederate army.

The Confederate defeat led to the passage of the Thirteenth Amendment to the Constitution, which abolished slavery.

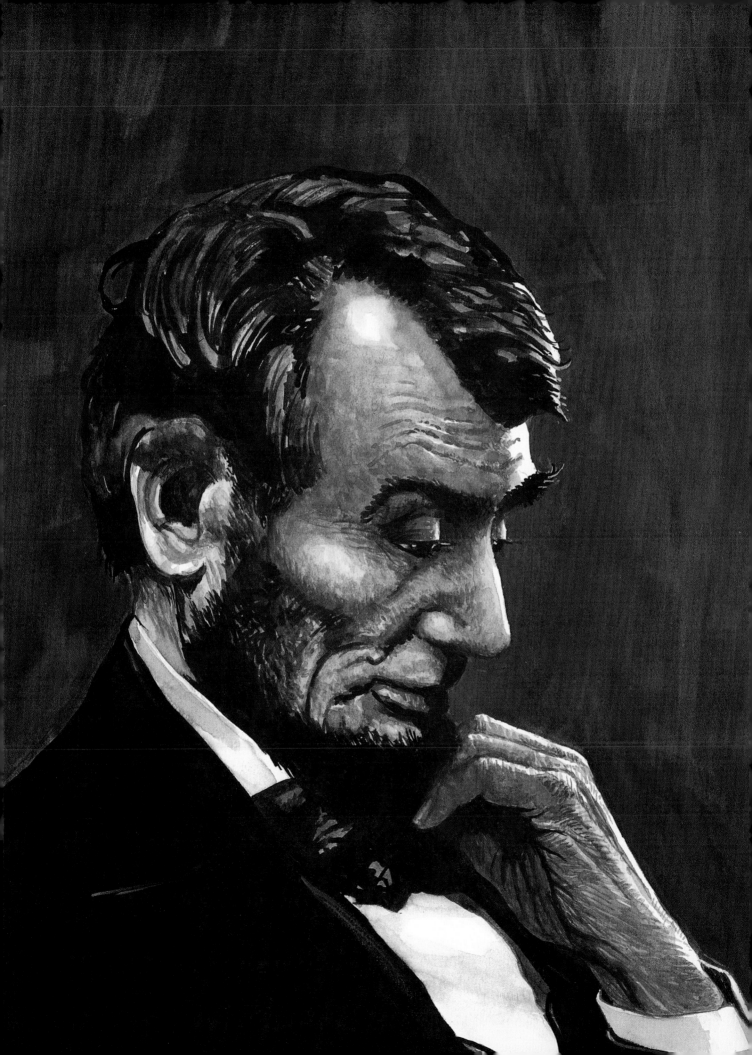

Elijah Lovejoy
(1802–1837)

"I have sworn eternal opposition to slavery and by the blessing of God I will never turn back."

*—from Lovejoy's speech to the mob in Alton, Illinois,
November 3, 1837*

Elijah Lovejoy was the publisher of an antislavery newspaper in Missouri, a slave state—a state that still allowed slavery. In 1836, after an angry proslavery mob destroyed his printing press, he moved across the Mississippi River to Alton, Illinois, a free state in which slavery was outlawed. There he continued to publish his views. "The truth is," he said, "that if you give ground a single inch, there is no stopping place."

"I know that you can tar and feather me, hang me up," he told a group in Alton. "If the civil authorities refuse to protect me, I must look to God."

On November 7, 1837, a new printing press was delivered to Lovejoy to replace the previous ones that had been destroyed by proslavery mobs. That night twenty men attacked, threw the press into the river, and killed Elijah Lovejoy.

Lucretia Mott
(1793–1880)

"Terrible as war must ever be, let us hope it will not be stayed by any compromise which shall continue the unequal, cruel war on the rights and liberties of millions of our unoffending fellow beings."
—*from a letter by Mott in* National Anti-Slavery Standard, *1861*

Lucretia Mott helped found the American Anti-Slavery Society and the Philadelphia Female Anti-Slavery Society. At an antislavery convention she helped organize, speakers were attacked and the building in which they spoke was burned. But Lucretia Mott refused to be silenced. "If our principles are right," she said, "why should we be cowards?"

"I was amazed to hear Mrs. Mott spoken of as a dangerous woman," the renowned advocate of women's rights and abolitionist Elizabeth Cady Stanton said of her friend. "Again and again I was warned against her influence. She was spoken of as an infidel, a heretic, a disturber who had destroyed the peace."

In 1848 Mott and Stanton organized a women's rights convention at Seneca Falls, New York. It adopted a Declaration of Sentiments, which began, "We hold these truths to be self-evident; that all men and women are created equal." For Lucretia Mott that meant *all* men and women, whites *and* blacks.

Harriet Beecher Stowe
(1811–1896)

"Ain't I yer master? Didn't I pay down $1,200 cash …? Ain't yer mine, now, body and soul?"

—Simon Legree, the brutal master in Stowe's novel
Uncle Tom's Cabin, *1851*

In 1851 Harriet Beecher Stowe wrote the beginnings of what would be her greatest work, her novel of social protest, *Uncle Tom's Cabin*, which dramatized the horrors of slavery. She read it to her two youngest children and they cried.

Uncle Tom's Cabin was first published one chapter at a time in a weekly magazine. In 1852 it came out in book form. Soon eight printing presses were kept running day and night to fulfill the demand for the book. It was translated into thirty languages.

Stowe's novel stirred up such antislavery feeling that it has long been listed as one of the causes of the Civil War, even by President Lincoln. In 1862, when he met Stowe, Lincoln said to her, "You're the little woman who made this great war!"

Charles Sumner
(1811–1874)

"Where slavery is, there liberty cannot be. Where liberty is, there slavery cannot be."
—from a speech Sumner made before Congress, 1864

Senator Charles Sumner of Massachusetts was a brilliant speaker and the leader of the antislavery movement in Congress. "All according to law," he decried that slaves were "branded like a mule, yoked like an ox, maimed like a cur, and constantly beaten." He called slavery "a sin . . . a 'national evil.'"

He was harsh on his proslavery colleagues, and two days after a particularly strong 1856 speech, a South Carolina member of the House of Representatives stormed into the Senate. He hit Sumner on the head with his cane again and again until Sumner fell to the floor, bloodied and unconscious.

During the three years it took Sumner to regain his health, the people of Massachusetts left Sumner's Senate seat empty, a tribute to his heroism. In 1859 Sumner returned and delivered a four-hour speech, "The Barbarism of Slavery"—a clear sign he would not be silenced.

Sojourner Truth
(1797–1883)

I am pleading for my people,
A poor downtrodden race,
Who dwell in freedom's boasted land,
With no abiding place . . .
Whilst I bear upon my body
The scars of many a gash,
I am pleading for my people
Who groan beneath the lash.
—from a hymn Truth wrote and recited at an 1850 meeting

Sojourner Truth, who ran to her freedom in 1826, hated what slavery had done to her family.

In 1843 Truth left New York and went west. She traveled thousands of miles, across many states, and wherever she went she spoke against slavery and for the rights of women.

"Do you think your talk about slavery does any good?" a listener at one of her talks asked. "Why, I don't care any more for your talk than I do for the bite of a flea." Truth answered, "The good Lord willing, I'll keep you scratching."

"Americans!, We hear your boasts of liberty," she wrote in her autobiography. "Your assertions that all men are created equal . . . hypocrites! liars! . . . dooming a sixth portion of your immense population to beastly servitude!"

In 1864 Truth met President Lincoln and told him, "I never heard of you before you were talked of for president."

"Well, I heard of you," he replied, "years and years before I even thought of being president."

People all across the United States had heard of Sojourner Truth. She got many of them scratching for abolition.

Harriet Tubman
(1820 or 1821–1913)

"I can't die but once."

*—on the risks Tubman took during her many sojourns
on the Underground Railroad, recalled in an interview
probably given in the early 1860s*

"I had a right to liberty or death," former slave Harriet Tubman once said. "If I could not have one, I would have the other."

In 1849 Tubman ran from her master's Maryland property to the house of a white woman she knew who hated slavery. From there she went from one safe house to the next. She was on the Underground Railroad. "I had crossed the line. I was *free*," but her parents, sisters, brothers, and friends were still slaves. "I was free," she decided, "and they should be free. I would make a home in the North and bring them there."

So Harriet Tubman went back. She risked her own freedom again and again as a "conductor" on the Underground Railroad.

Tubman made her trips in winter, when the nights were long and people stayed mostly indoors. With the stars to guide her, she helped more than three hundred slaves escape, and she never let them turn back. When some were scared, afraid to continue, she pointed a gun to their heads and they went on. Years later she said proudly, "I never ran my train off track. I never lost a passenger."

Nat Turner
(1800–1831)

"I am here loaded with chains, and willing to suffer the fait [sic] that awaits me."
—a statement made just before Turner's execution, 1831

As a child, Nat Turner felt he "was intended for some great purpose." He saw a vision of "white spirits and black spirits engaged in battle, and the sun was darkened, the thunder rolled in the heavens, and blood flowed in streams. . . . And by signs in the heavens, that it would make known to me when I should commence the great work."

On August 21, 1831, there was a solar eclipse, and Turner began his "great work": a slave rebellion. He and seven other slaves stormed their master's house, killed the family, took guns and horses, and moved on. Their battle spread as others joined them. By the second day, after more than fifty white people had been killed, the rebels were overpowered by a large force. More than one hundred blacks were killed—many who had nothing to do with the revolt. Turner himself was caught several weeks later and hanged. At his brief trial the judge told Nat Turner, "Your only hope must be in another world," and then pronounced his punishment, that Turner be "hung by the neck until you are dead! dead! dead!"

The revolt shook the South. It shattered the belief that black slaves wouldn't fight for their freedom.

Denmark Vesey
(1767?–1822)

"Liberty won by white men would lose half its luster. . . .
Who would be free, themselves must strike the blow. Better
even die free, than to live as slaves. . . . Remember Denmark
Vesey of Charleston."
> —*Frederick Douglass in an 1863 speech in Rochester,*
> *New York, urging blacks to join the Union army*

In 1800 Denmark Vesey, a slave, won a lottery and bought his freedom. He opened a carpentry shop in Charleston, South Carolina. Later, he became a church leader and often quoted the Bible: "He that stealeth a man, and selleth him, or if he be found in his hand, he shall surely be put to death."

Talk was not enough for Denmark Vesey.

Vesey planned a revolt for the second Monday in July 1822. According to some reports, several thousand slaves made knives, swords, and disguises to help in their escape. But they were betrayed and the plan discovered. Vesey and 130 other blacks were arrested. Thirty-five of them were hanged, including Denmark Vesey.

David Walker
(1785–1830)

"The Americans say we are ungrateful—but ask them, for heaven's sake, what we should be grateful to them for . . . murdering our fathers and mothers? . . . for chaining and handcuffing us, branding us, cramming fire down our throats, or for keeping us in slavery?"
—*from Walker's* Appeal in Four Articles IV, *1829*

David Walker was a black man born free in North Carolina. He traveled far from there, saw many places and many people, and wrote that slaves were "the most degraded, wretched, and abject sets of beings that ever lived since the world began." He moved north, to Boston, where he sold clothes and agitated for the abolition of slavery.

In 1829 Walker wrote a booklet declaring that America is "more our country than it is the whites'—we have enriched it with our blood and tears." Of whites he wrote, "Woe, woe will be to you if we have to obtain our freedom by fighting."

Walker despaired for America and for himself. "If I remain in this bloody land," he said, "I will not live long." He didn't. In June 1830 he was found dead. A price had already been put on his head. His supporters believed he had been poisoned.

Theodore Dwight Weld
(1803–1895)

"There is not a man on earth who does not believe slavery is a curse."

—*from Weld's* Slavery As It Is, *1839*

"Every man knows that slavery is a curse," Theodore Weld wrote with his wife in the introduction to their 1839 pamphlet, *Slavery As It Is.* "Whoever denies this . . . try him; clank the chains in his ears and tell him they are for *him*. Give him an hour to prepare his wife and children for a life of slavery. Bid him make haste and get ready their necks for the yoke, and their wrists for the coffle chains, then look at his pale lips and trembling knees, and you have *nature's* testimony against slavery."

Weld's wife was Angelina Grimké. She and her older sister, Sarah, were the first white Southern women to be counted among the nation's leading abolitionists. Weld and the Grimké sisters trained abolitionists, who spread their message throughout the country. "Slavery," in Angelina Grimké's words, "is a violation of the natural order of things, and no human power can much longer perpetuate it."

Source Notes

Each source note includes the first word or words and the last word or words of a quotation and its source. References are to books cited in the Selected Bibliography.

p. 5   "I, John Brown . . . but with blood.": Seldes, p. 118

p. 6   "I often . . . myself.": Douglass, p. 43; "tore off . . . switches.": Douglass, p. 56; "He was . . . heart.": Douglass, p. 41; "Go where . . . world," and "and you . . . without rival.": Douglass, pp. 434–435

p. 9   "Let all . . . tremble.": *Annals,* v. 5, p. 423; "In the . . . blood . . . I demand . . . soil.": *Harper's,* v. 4, p. 30; "I will . . . justice . . . I am . . . WILL BE HEARD. . . . an earthquake . . . Death and Hell.": *Annals,* v. 5, p. 423

p. 10 "I do order . . . shall be, free.": *Annals,* v. 9, p. 399; "A house divided . . . cannot stand . . . I believe . . . half free.": *Annals,* v. 9, p. 1; "There is no reason . . . happiness.": *Annals,* v. 9, pp. 11–12; "I hold that . . . Constitution . . . the Union . . . is perpetual.": *Annals,* v. 9, p. 252

p. 12 "I have . . . turn back.": Seldes, p. 440; "The truth is . . . stopping place.": Gabriel, p. 241; "I know . . . hang me up . . . If the civil . . . look to God.": Ruchames, p. 141

p. 15 "Terrible as war . . . fellow beings.": Bacon, p. 180; "If our . . . right . . . why . . . be cowards?": Bacon, p. 57; "I was amazed . . . peace.": Frost, p. 66; "When the true . . . was Lucretia Mott.": Sterling, p. 200; "We hold . . . created equal.": Bacon, p. 127

p. 16 "Ain't . . . body and soul?": Stowe, *Uncle Tom's Cabin,* Paul S. Eriksson, New York, 1964, pp. 452–453; "You're . . . this great war!": Hedrick, p. vii

p. 19 "Where slavery is . . . cannot be.": Seldes, p. 667; "All according to law . . . branded . . . beaten. . . . a sin . . . evil.'": Donald, p. 355

p. 20 "I am . . . the lash.": McKissack, *Sojourner Truth,* p. 102; "Do you . . . any good? . . . Why, I don't care . . . a flea. . . . The good . . . scratching.": McKissack, *Sojourner Truth,* p. 119; "Americans! . . . liberty . . . Your assertions . . . servitude!": Pauli, p. 162; "I never . . . for president . . . Well . . . you . . . years and years . . . being president.": Pauli, p. 145

p. 23 "I can't die but once.": Blassingame, p. 459; "I had the right . . . death . . . If I . . . the other.": King, p. 61; "I had . . . was *free* . . . I was free . . . bring them there.": Partnow, p. 183; "I never . . . passenger.": King, p. 61

p. 24 "I am . . . awaits me.": *Annals,* v. 5, p. 479; "was intended . . . purpose. . . . white spirits . . . great work.": *Annals,* v. 5, pp. 472–474; "Your only . . . another world . . . hung . . . dead! dead! dead!": *Annals,* v. 5, p. 481

p. 27 "Liberty . . . of Charleston.": Douglass, pp. 779–780; "He that stealeth . . . to death.": Exodus, 21:16

p. 28 "The Americans . . . in slavery?": King, p. 30; "the most . . . world began.": Fishel, p. 148; "more our country . . . and tears.": Wilson, p. 102; "Woe, woe . . . by fighting.": Franklin, p. 189; "If I remain . . . land . . . I . . . not live long.": McKissack, *Rebels Against Slavery,* p. 88

p. 31 "There is not . . . a curse.": Ruchames, p. 165; "Every man . . . curse . . . Whoever . . . against slavery.": Ruchames, p. 165; "Slavery . . . is a violation . . . perpetuate it.": Partnow, p. 781

Selected Bibliography

Annals of America. London: Encyclopaedia Britannica, 1968.

Bacon, Margaret Hope. *Valiant Friend: The Life of Lucretia Mott.* New York: Walker, 1980.

Bayliss, John F., ed. *Black Slave Narratives.* New York: Macmillan, 1970.

Bennett, Lerone, Jr. *Pioneers in Protest.* Chicago: Johnson, 1968.

Bergman, Peter M. *The Chronological History of the Negro in America.* New York: Harper, 1969.

Blassingame, John W., ed. *Slave Testimony.* Baton Rouge: Louisiana State University Press, 1977.

Boyer, Richard O. *The Legend of John Brown.* New York: Knopf, 1973.

Donald, David. *Charles Sumner and the Coming of the Civil War.* New York: Knopf, 1960.

Douglass, Frederick. *Autobiographies.* New York: The Library of America, 1994.

Dudley, William. *Slavery: Opposing Viewpoints.* San Diego: Greenhaven Press, 1992.

Fishel, Leslie H., Jr., and Benjamin Quarles. *The Negro American: A Documentary History.* New York: Morrow, 1967.

Franklin, John Hope. *From Slavery to Freedom.* New York: Knopf, 1974.

Frost, Elizabeth, and Kathryn Cullen-DuPont. *Women's Suffrage in America.* New York: Facts on File, 1992.

Gabriel, Ralph Henry. *Pageant of America,* vol. 2. New Haven: Yale, 1928.

Harper's Encyclopedia of United States History. New York: Harper & Brothers, 1907.

Hart, Albert Bushnell, ed. *American History Told by Contemporaries.* New York: Macmillan, 1964.

Hedrick, Joan D. *Harriet Beecher Stowe: A Life.* New York: Oxford University Press, 1994.

King, Anita, ed. *Quotations in Black.* Westport, Conn.: Greenwood Press, 1981.

Mayer, Henry. *All On Fire: William Lloyd Garrison and the Abolition of Slavery.* New York: St. Martin's, 1998.

McKissack, Patricia C., and Fredrick L. McKissack. *Rebels Against Slavery: American Slave Revolts.* New York: Scholastic, 1996.

McKissack, Patricia C., and Fredrick McKissack. *Sojourner Truth: Ain't I a Woman?* New York: Scholastic, 1992.

Partnow, Elaine, ed. *The New Quotable Woman.* New York: Facts on File, 1992.

Pauli, Hertha. *Her Name Was Sojourner Truth.* New York: Appleton-Century-Crofts, 1962.

Ruchames, Louis. *The Abolitionists.* New York: Putnam, 1963.

Seldes, George, ed. *The Great Quotations.* New York: Lyle Stuart, 1966.

Sterling, Dorothy. *Lucretia Mott: Gentle Warrior.* New York: Doubleday, 1964.

Stern, Philip Van Doren, ed. *The Annotated Uncle Tom's Cabin.* New York: Paul S. Eriksson, 1964.

Wilson, Ruth. *Our Blood and Tears: Black Freedom Fighters.* New York: Putnam, 1972.

Woodson, Carter G., and Charles H. Wesley. *The Negro in Our History.* Washington, D.C.: Associated Publishers, 1962.